2.5

123920

Pebble® Plus

MILITARY BRANCHES

# THE U.S. MARINE CORPS

by Jennifer Reed

Consulting Editor: Gail Saunders-Smith, PhD

Capstone
press®

Mankato, Minnesota

Pebble Plus is published by Capstone Press,
151 Good Counsel Drive, P.O. Box 669, Mankato, Minnesota 56002.
www.capstonepress.com

1 2 3 4 5 6 13 12 11 10 09 08

*Library of Congress Cataloging-in-Publication Data*
Reed, Jennifer, 1967 –
    The U.S. Marine Corps / By Jennifer Reed.
    p. cm. — (Pebble plus. Military branches)
    Includes bibliographical references and index.
    ISBN-13: 978-1-4296-1735-2 (hardcover)
    ISBN-10: 1-4296-1735-7 (hardcover)
    1.  United States. Marine Corps — Juvenile literature.  I. Title. II. Series.
VE23.R44 2009
359.9'60973 — dc22                                    2008001750

Summary: Simple text and photographs describe the U.S. Marine Corps' purpose, jobs, machines, and tools.

**Editorial Credits**
Gillia Olson, editor; Renée T. Doyle, designer; Jo Miller, photo researcher


**Photo Credits**
Capstone Press/Karon Dubke, 3
DVIC/CPL Robert R. Attebury, 17; LCPL Michael L. Haas, 11; MC2(SW/AW) Elizabeth Merriam, 13; PHAA
      Shannon K. Garcia, 5
Getty Images Inc./David Greedy, 19; Science Faction/Ed Darack, 15
Photo by Ted Carlson/Fotodynamics, 9, 21
Shutterstock/Philip Lange, 1
U.S. Navy Photo by JO2 Zack Baddorf, 7; by PHAA Shannon Garcia, cover (front and back), 22


**Artistic Effects**
Shutterstock/iNNOCENt (white sand), cover (front and back), 1, 24
iStockphoto/James Kingman (metal in title), cover (front and back), 1

## Note to Parents and Teachers

The Military Branches set supports national science standards related to science, technology, and society. This book describes and illustrates the U.S. Marine Corps. The images support early readers in understanding the text. The repetition of words and phrases helps early readers learn new words. This book also introduces early readers to subject-specific vocabulary words, which are defined in the Glossary section. Early readers may need assistance to read some words and to use the Table of Contents, Glossary, Read More, Internet Sites, and Index sections of the book.

# Table of Contents

# What Is the Marine Corps?

The Marine Corps is
a branch of the
United States Armed Forces.
Marines are often the first
to fight for the country.

# Marine Corps Jobs

Marines are trained
to fight anywhere.
They fight on land,
at sea, or in the air.

Marine pilots fly airplanes
and helicopters.
They use F/A-18 airplanes
to attack enemy targets.

MARINE OF OTR
CPL K E GARCIA

121

9

Marines have other jobs too.

Mechanics fix machines.

Reporters write Marine news.

# Machines and Tools

Marines use vehicles
to get to their targets.
The AAV can float on water
and drive on land.

Big helicopters carry
Marines into battle.
The Sea Knight is
a Marine helicopter.

Marines also have weapons.

Each Marine carries

an M-16 rifle.

Grenades and missiles

blow up enemy targets.

Marines carry binoculars
to see faraway things.
They use binoculars
and other tools
to find out about enemies.

# Keeping Us Safe

The brave Marines
work together.
They are always ready
to protect the country.

# Glossary

**AAV** — Assault Amphibian Vehicle; AAVs can float on water and travel on land.

**Armed Forces** — the whole military; the U.S. Armed Forces include the Army, Navy, Air Force, Marine Corps, and Coast Guard.

**branch** — a part of a larger group

**grenade** — a small weapon used to blow up a target; grenades are thrown by a person or fired by a gun.

**mechanic** — a person who fixes machines

**missile** — a weapon that is fired at a target to blow it up

**rifle** — a weapon that can fire bullets very fast

**target** — an object at which to aim or shoot

**vehicle** — a machine that carries people and goods

# Read More

**Hamilton, John**. *The Marine Corps.* Defending the Nation. Edina, Minn.: Abdo, 2007.

**Kaelberer, Angie Peterson**. *U.S. Marine Corps Assault Vehicles.* Military Vehicles. Mankato, Minn.: Capstone Press, 2007.

**Rustad, Martha E. H.** *U.S. Marine Corps Combat Jets.* Military Vehicles. Mankato, Minn.: Capstone Press, 2007.

# Internet Sites

FactHound offers a safe, fun way to find Internet sites related to this book. All of the sites on FactHound have been researched by our staff.

Here's how:

1. Visit *www.facthound.com*

2. Choose your grade level.

3. Type in this book ID **1429617357** for age-appropriate sites. You may also browse subjects by clicking on letters, or by clicking on pictures and words.

4. Click on the **Fetch It** button.

**FactHound will fetch the best sites for you!**

# Index

Word Count: 143
Grade: 1
Early-Intervention Level: 22